# Ghosts of Yorkshire

# Ghosts of Yorkshire

by

W. R. Mitchell

DALESMAN BOOKS
1987

The Dalesman Publishing Company Ltd.,
Clapham, via Lancaster, LA2 8EB.

First published in this format 1982
Second edition 1987

ISBN: 0 85206 886 7

Printed in Great Britain by Fretwell & Cox Limited, Goulbourne Street, Keighley,
West Yorkshire BD21 1PZ.

# Contents



Cover design by E. Jeffrey.

Drawings in the text by Janet Acland, Stanley Bond, Edward Gower, Fred Lawson and P. B. Rennison.

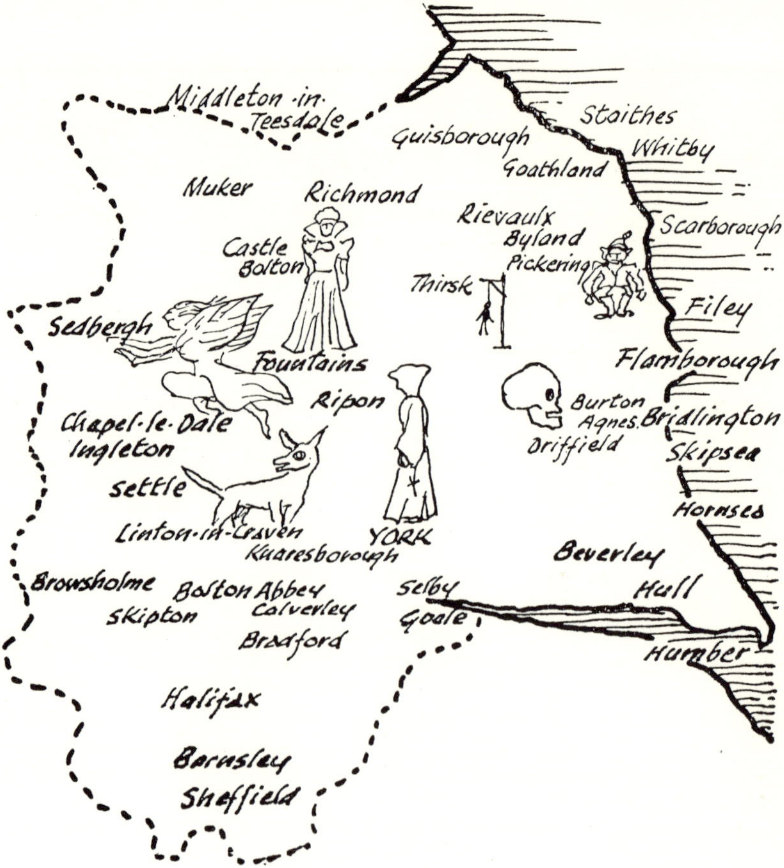


# Ghostly Yorkshire

# Preface

MOST of us enjoy tales of the paranormal — of inexplicable sights, smells and 'things that go bump in the night.' We do not mind being scared — if we are in the security of our own homes.

Years ago, warmed by a fire that sent fingers of light flickering across a darkened room, family groups revelled in the gloom, the howling of a wind in the chimney and in the story-teller's solemn narrative. Radio and television have taken over his role.

Our homes may be snug and centrally heated, ablaze with electric light, but radio and television writers and producers are masters at creating the eerie atmosphere for ghost stories. Television in particular, demanding total concentration, is the modern equivalent of the old teller of tales. The cunningly-contrived settings, with their creaking doors and stairs, wind effects and cobwebs produced synthetically (they have never seen a spider!) make our hands clammy and chill our spines.

A well-presented television ghost story closes the credibility gap. In the cold light of day there are a few 'don't knows.' A person either believes in ghosts, or laughs when ghosts are mentioned. The non-believer claims that 'it's all in the mind,' which (he asserts) can conjure up ghosts — even 'voices.' So far even the most devout believers in ghosts have not produced incontrovertible proof of their existence. We are surrounded by a haze of superstition.

Specialists make a distinction between a ghost and a spirit. A ghost is nebulous — it can be seen through — but a spirit appears solid and is usually dressed in the clothes of its time. In this book the word 'ghost' has been generally used.

Believers in the supernatural say that a person can be aware of a ghostly presence but see nothing. There may be the sound of footsteps or simply an aroma. At one Yorkshire house, on a monastic site, people have detected smells which would have been familiar to the monks. The smells were of incense, mead and ale, and onions. Colours are associated with particular moods — blue for happiness, red for anger or fear, green for jealousy or envy.

A folk-lore aspect of ghosts is worthy of study. The ghost with its head tucked underneath its arm, an old theme, is doubtless a version of some old head cult. Was not a fairy dislike for metal that sort of dislike a Stone Age man might feel on meeting newcomers able to work iron? Apparitions reported at wells, rivers or potholes may be traditions harking back to a primitive worship of nature spirits.

*Ghosts of Yorkshire,* a successor to *Haunted Yorkshire* and *Yorkshire Ghosts,* is an entertainment, not a critical study of its subject. It is far from exhaustive. For every Yorkshire ghost story preserved, scores must have been forgotten. They formed part of an extensive oral tradition, only a small fraction of which was written down.

Stories about ghosts proliferated during the 17th and 18th centuries and possibly reached their highest point of appreciation in the early 19th century. Then, with a scientific and technological revolution, attempts were made to assert some control over the spirit world, by seances and other formal occasions. We live in a period of time characterised by great cynicism. Many people, regularly absorbing a ration of horrific tales, via the mass media, tend to think of ghosts as part of the entertainment industry.

In *Ghosts of Yorkshire* I deal with the old, well-loved Yorkshire, with its curious, eccentric boundary, rather than the new, squared up Yorkshire left after the re-organisation of local government in April 1974. Some of the ghosts were, alas, transferred to neighbouring counties. I hope those counties are cherishing them!

**"I've left mine at home. I'd a frightful headache"**

# 1 A Bevy of Fairies

FAIRIES, inhabiting the remoter parts of the Yorkshire Dales, avoided the exposed areas, where gossamer wings might be shredded by strong winds. They also kept away from bogs and marshy valley bottoms where clothes of delicate green would be spattered by peat or mud. A fairy preferred the sheltered middle reaches of the valleys, especially areas of conical hills. Here, at a respectable distance from farms and villages, 'wee folk' danced at night to the sweet music of pipes.

But who first cut the fairies down to size? Who provided them with gossamer wings and ballet dresses? The word 'faerie' is derived from a terrain — from fairyland indeed — and fairies were at first full-sized people. They may have been a little larger than life size. A witch might be called a fairy, and often was. During the course of 200 or 300 years, fairies have become glittering midgets with wands.

The fairies of Middleton-in-Teesdale belong to County Durham, but until government re-organisation could be partly claimed by Yorkshire because they washed their clothes in the river that here formed the county boundary! Fairies danced on Tower Hill, and it was claimed that the sound of the pipes might be heard by anyone placing an ear close to the ground. A Middleton woman saw a fairy — a small girl with bright red eyes and a dress of green. Teesdale mothers placed knives in the cots of their children as a deterrent to fairies.

Most Teesdale people were aware of fairies because they feared an aquatic variety, Peg Powler, who drowned at least one person a year in a river of unpredictable moods. When storms broke over Cross Fell, and the Tees was in spate, the swirling yellow patches of foam in the river were called 'Peg Powler's Suds'. Formations in millstone grit by the river at Cotherstones were called Fairy Cupboards.

Kelpie, who lived on the Muker stretch of the Swale, sometimes bewitched humans. When a farmer, Edward Cleasby, walked towards the river one night and did not return, the locals were sure that the Kelpie had taken him.

Wharfedale's profusion of ghost stories is explained in part by the presence of writers of whimsical happenings, such as J. H. Dixon and Halliwell Sutcliffe. Fairies were seen by Daniel Cooper near Kilnsey. One moonlight night he walked from the village, using a path across the fields and saw fairies dancing in a pasture. Cooper rented that field and so he had a territorial interest in the fairy dance. He returned next morning and found mushrooms. Naturally he believed that he had mistaken mushrooms for fairies, but his old aunt declared: 'My dear, you saw the fairies and the mushrooms were a gift to you because you were good and did not disturb the dance.'

The belief in fairies was fairly strong in the Dales when Dixon wrote over 80 years ago, 'but it is by no means so prevalent as it was.' The late Francis King (known as the Craven Minstrel because he played a fiddle at dances and other social events) firmly believed in fairies. He had seen their 'gambols' in Lothersdale. 'As poor King was almost blind, even believers in fairies must receive his testimony *cum grano salis,'* commented Dixon who, however, was fascinated by the subject.

The Craven fairies were accused of kidnapping children, leaving one of their own in place of a stolen child.

Elbolton, one of the Wharfedale reef knolls, near the hamlet of Thorpe, is still a perfect setting for fairies. A Wharfedale man saw them dancing on a moonlit night. Fairies sometimes invited a spectator to join their dance, and the invitation must not be refused. This observer had been drinking hard. He forced a song upon them and the fairies kicked and pinched him. As he staggered away he caught a fairy and put it in his pocket. The fairy escaped before he got home. Neighbours put the whole incident down to 'the ale talking'.

Fairy Hole, in Upper Wharfedale, was described by the topographer Harry Speight as 'a low opening in the limestone which can only properly be entered by such tiny sprites as fairies. Ordinary mortals must descend to an access on all fours.'

True to form, the Airedale fairies resided in the more sheltered middle reaches of the valleys. They were seen at Cottingley, near Bingley. Sir Arthur Conan Doyle, the writer, believed in fairies; his belief may have been strengthened by Frances Griffiths, aged ten, who spent the summer of 1917 at Cottingley with the Wrights and their daughter Elsie, aged 13.

The girls not only saw fairies in the wood at the back of Lynwood Terrace; they photographed them. Not many people believed there were fairies at the bottom of the garden, but no one could disprove the story. Frances returned to Cottingley in the summers of 1920 and 1921, and again photographs featuring fairies were taken. Conan Doyle and a Mr. Gardner wrote about the fairies in the *Strand Magazine* for Christmas 1920.

A number of large 'fairy rings' might be found in the parish of Danby, on the north-eastern moors. The parish clerk told Canon Atkinson that children ran round the rings, but never quite ten times, which would have given the fairies power over them, 'and they would have come and taken us away for good to go and live where they lived.'

A domestic form of fairy — a brownie, or hob — generally gave help to hard-pressed humans. The lady at Sturfitt Hall, near Reeth, rewarded her hob by offering a new suit of clothes but this was the most effective way of getting a hob to leave. She never saw this member of her staff again. When a hob was not wanted in Arkengarthdale, a woman despatched it by producing a Bible and a candle into which she had stuck pins. The little chap fled in the form of a grey cat; as a cat, indeed, he might have been more useful!

A hob seen on the Ingleton–Hawes road became known as Lile Hob of Blea Moor. He waited between Newby Head and Gearstones and when a cart came level with him he jumped on to it for a short ride. A newcomer to the district, perturbed by the hob, rushed into the house at Newby Head and said he had seen a ghost. A man laughed and explained: 'Why'a, it were nobbut Lile Hob.'

This supernatural being of Blea Moor vanished on the day that Jack Sunter, a Dentdale shepherd, saw three rings sticking from the side of a moss. He twirled them on his stick and one flew off and was not found again. The other rings were sold to a gamekeeper called Prior, whose wife cleaned them up and saw they were armlets made of silver, inlaid with enamel. The rings were sold at Kirkby Lonsdale; with their removal from Blea Moor, Lile Hob departed.

A hob who lived at Close House, near Skipton, threshed the corn and helped with haymaking. When the hob was given a red hood he cleared off. The north-eastern moorland area is true hob country. The hob of Hart Hall, Glaisdale End, helped in the hayfield, with corn threshing, or turned up when a wain had become bogged down in mud and had to be shifted by hand. The farmer and his family, stirring in their beds, sometimes heard the thump of the flail against wood in the barn as the hob threshed grain after normal hours. Someone saw the hob and noticed his shabby clothes; he was 'amaist as nakt as when he wur boorn.' A warm garment was made for him, and the hob left Hart Hall.

Farndale's hob favoured a tumulus called Obtrush, near a line of scarps on Rudland Moor. Leyland explained that Obtrush or Obtrush Roque means Hob Thrush Ruck (or heap). The Farndale sprite, Hob o' th' Hursts, was peevish and became a nuisance to the farmer at the nearest holding. This man did not think to provide the hob with new clothes, a sure way of getting rid of him; instead he decided to leave the farm for another one. Early one morning the farmer piled his possessions on a horse-drawn cart and set off down the dale. A neighbour observed: 'Ah see thou's flittin'!' Before the farmer could reply, hob stuck his head from a churn and said: 'Aye, we'se flittin'!' The farmer wearily turned the horse and cart and returned to his old home!

Sea-carved caves in Runswick Bay were called Hob Holes. The hob cured whooping cough. At low water, a mother would carry her child to the mouth of his cave and invoke its tenant.

Country folk tended to blame the supernatural for any calamity for which there was no easy explanation. Among the impish, even malicious creatures, was the troll, a cave-dweller who wandered about at night. If he was in the open at dawn he was turned into stone. The King of the Trolls presided over a subterranean palace, adorned with stalactites, encrusted with jewels. A troll was a product of Norse imagination, and varied in appearance depending in which area of Scandinavia he developed. The Danish trolls were fatter, pleasanter and more jolly than their Norwegian cousins. It has been suggested that trolls gave their names to Trollers Gill, near Appletreewick.

# 2. Haunted Halls

A CONSIDERABLE number of Yorkshire ghost stories relate to old halls, in which (popularly) every other panel is hollow, leading to a secret passage; every third step on the staircase creaks, attic windows are frequently banging whenever there is a wind, and there are screams from the tower.

Secret rooms there were — hidey holes for Catholic priests at times of religious intolerance — and it is possible that, when they were being made in secret, odd sounds were heard at night. The householder would explain the noises to his startled servants as being made by a ghost.

Mary Queen of Scots is said to have spent two nights at Nappa Hall, in Wensleydale, with the Metcalfes; she was certainly held captive in the valley for a few months at Bolton Castle. A visitor to Nappa Hall in 1878 saw an apparition of the Queen in the hall.

Two other female ghosts from Wensleydale were those of an unknown woman at Countersett Hall, which stands not far from Semerwater, and a grey lady at Stalling Busk.

Down in mid-Airedale, a 'little fellow wearing breeches' moved from room to room at one hall, and set alight material laid in grates. This was in a period before massive industrialisation — a time that can be vividly recalled at the National Trust property of East Riddlesden Hall, on the Bradford side of Keighley. Early in the 17th century the hall was occupied by the Rishworths, whose children were rocked in a carved wooden cradle (still in one of the bedrooms). On New Year's Eve it rocks without being touched by a visible being. Maybe the ghost of Riddlesden's Grey Lady (another phenomenon) pushes the cradle.

Airedale had two Grey Ladies — at Riddlesden and Gawthorpe Hall, Bingley. An account of the second gives a hint of the nature of the first. Gawthorpe's haunting was by a nun believed to have been murdered by her lover (tut tut!). She was described by a householder as being cloaked and hooded. The figure moved across the driveway in front of him.

An unexpected tang of the sea occurred in the ghost annals of Bradford with the story of a murdered admiral who stumped up and down the Paper Hall, a building that has become derelict. Paper Hall now stands behind a row of shops at the top of Church Bank. Seen outside the hall by a startled pedestrian was a man in shining white armour. He was 'whistling a happy tune and swaying to and fro holding a spear in his hand'.

A girl clad in white gave extra distinction to Bolling Hall, at Bradford. Formerly the home of the Bollings and the Tempests, it is now owned by West Yorkshire and the public has regular access. The White Girl saved

**Nappa Hall, Wensleydale, where was seen the ghost of Mary Queens of Scots**

Bradford when it was besieged by Royalists in 1643. The Earl of Newcastle, annoyed at the townsfolk's resistance to Royalist force, commanded that next day his soldiers 'should put to the sword every man, woman and child without regard to age or distinction whatsoever . . .' The Earl spent the night at Bolling Hall. He slept badly. Three times the clothes were pulled from his bed and the White Girl wailed : 'Pity poor Bradford.' Sceptics said that the Earl was drunk. Cruder folk suggested that the girl was not a ghost but a venturesome local maid. However, the Earl cancelled the previous day's order, and the people of Bradford were spared.

Children visiting the churchyard at Calverley, near Leeds, formed a circle, joined hands and sang:

*Old Calverley, old Calverley, I'll have thee by the ears,*
*I'll cut thee into collops unless thee appear.*

They daringly tried to conjure up the spirit of Walter Calverley, who nearly succeeded in killing all the members of his family. Walter's crime was committed early in the 17th century. Already, for about 500 years, his family had been lords of the manor of Calverley and Pudsey, the occupants of Calverley Hall, and they were generally respected. Walter, after initial promise, degenerated; he drank, and gambled to excess and revelled in anything with a touch of evil about it. Inevitably he faced financial ruin. In

1605 he turned on his wife, a South Country woman, and accused her of being unfaithful. The more she protested she was innocent, the graver did his charges become. Walter, in short, developed an unreasonable hatred, possibly because his wife had pleaded with him to mend his ways and offered to sell her jewels to meet his debts.

Walter Calverley's brother was at university: a university friend came to Calverley Hall to ask for monetary help, and this was Walter's moment of crisis. He 'retires himself into a gallery, when being alone he fell into a deep consideration of his state, how his prodigall course of life had wronged his brother, abused his wife and undone his children, and the misery he should leave his children in.' One of his three children, aged four, ran into the gallery, and Walter slew the child with his dagger. He lifted up the bleeding body and carried it into the presence of his wife and the second child. Then he wounded his wife on the shoulder and killed the infant.

Only his son, Henry, remained alive, and he was 'a brait at nurse' staying at Norton. Walter set off on horseback to murder again. The horse, driven hard, fell and rolled on to him. Before he could resume the journey he was overpowered and taken to Wakefield. Here his wife magnanimously forgave him.

Walter's life ended at York, but the journey from Wakefield was delayed for some months because the plague was raging. He was convicted and sentenced to death by pressing. Weights would be set upon his body until the life was crushed from him. Towards the end of this terrible ordeal, Walter pleaded with a servant to add the last weight and thus end his life quickly. The servant obliged — and was hung by the indignant authorities. Calverley did not plead at his trial and his estates were therefore not confiscated.

The body of Walter Calverley was buried at St. Mary's, Castlegate, York, but his remains may have been moved to Calverley in secret. Hence the old sport of baiting 'Owd Calverley' enjoyed by local children. His ghost was usually seen at night, mounted on a horse without a head. Walter also strode down a corridor at the hall which was later bricked up. A parson staying at the hall, after a preaching appointment, had his night's sleep disturbed three times when he was inexplicably tossed on to the floor.

The 'last mad freak of the ghost of poor Walter Calverley' was the ringing of the bell in the church tower at 1 a.m. The bell tolled for a long time because the key to the tower could not be found immediately. When the key was found, the bells stopped ringing.

Three ghosts inhabited Hawksworth Hall, near Guiseley. A negro page boy sneaked into one of the bedrooms and left the imprint of his hand upon a pillow; a ghostly lady left doors open all over the house, and a cowled monk prowled through the corridors and galleries.

A psychic research specialist spent a night in Bolling Hall in the 1920s and had an undisturbed vigil. Did he also hope to see the ghost of Richard Oastler, the 'factory king'? Oastler used to visit the Walkers at Bolling Hall and he threatened to haunt the place after his death if the Walkers' son did not change his mind and believe in a future life. Oastler died on August 22, 1861; that morning his ghost appeared before the son of the house. Another sighting at Bolling is of the distressed figure of a woman standing on the roof and looking out towards Tong Hall.

Oakwell Hall, near Batley, had a bloody footprint associated with William Batt, a member of the family who built the hall in 1683 and lived here until 1747. This hall featured in the Brontë story. As a school for young ladies it was known to Charlotte, who called it Fieldhead in her novel *Shirley*. The William Batt of footprint fame was murdered by a Mr. Greame of Barnet on December 30, 1684. His ghost was seen at Oakwell that day, arriving on horseback and visiting the main bedroom. The footprint remained as though to confirm the visit.

Ghosts have been commonplace at Temple Newsam, the mansion owned by Leeds and annually visited by large numbers of people. When it was a private house, Lord Halifax attempted to get to sleep here on a winter night in 1908. At about 12-15 a.m. the firelight revealed what he thought was a woman in blue; she crossed the bedroom and went into the Damask Dressing Room. The ghost, seen by others, is of an elderly woman. A lace shawl is draped over her blue gown. The Red Room is also haunted; screams as from someone in agony have been heard in this part of the south wing. A small boy haunting the Darnley Room in the north wing has been seen stepping out of a cupboard. In the same room the apparition of a Knight Templar has been observed.

A bedroom at Temple Newsam, known today as Room No. 4, has a door which opens and closes for no reason. People occupying the room have heard loud noises, similar to those when heavy furniture is moved from the floor below, a phenomenon called the Phantom Ball. A man and his wife who stood in the Long Gallery at Temple Newsam saw a figure wearing a brown habit emerge from one of the doors and enter the chapel, crossing it towards the organ and then vanishing. During the 1939–45 war a man on the staff saw a 'kind of mist, a film' in the Long Gallery.

A ghost haunting the grounds of Potternewton Hall, Leeds, drove around the house in a carriage-and-four but was not heard again after some elm trees were felled. This suggests that people heard the sound of wind among the branches and used their imagination.

Bramham Park, near Wetherby, has the sound of galloping hooves, supposed to be fleeing from the Battle of Bramham Moor in 1304. They were reputed to have been heard by Col. Lane Fox, who held open a gate for them in the mistaken belief that the Bramham Moor Hounds were on their way to join him at a meet.

The ghost of Lady Margaret haunted a six-chimneyed house in Kirkgate, Wakefield. Someone locked her in one of the cramped little attics high under the chimneys and they forgot all about her.

The tread of ghostly boots has been heard in the upper corridor of Crawthorne Hall, Greetland, near Halifax. An owner of the building was keen on hunting. A pack of hounds was kennelled in the orchard. He was challenged to visit the hounds, dressed in ordinary clothes, at night, and he obliged. The man was not seen again, but his riding boots lay in the kennels.

Lady Bolles, of Heath Old Hall, near Wakefield, died in 1662, aged 83.

She had thought a good deal about her coming death and left £700 to be spent on mourning and £400 to cover funeral expenses. Her will detailed the spending of a further £120 so that open house could be kept for six weeks. Lady Bolles had conquered a gambling urge, and the room set aside for it was walled up. After her death the room was opened again, but some of her other wishes were not honoured, so Lady Bolles returned to haunt the place, favouring the banqueting hall at Christmas. Her restless being was laid at a hole in the river called Bolles Pit.

Newburgh Priory, near Coxwold, had the ghost of a man wearing silk breeches and powdered wig, which suggests an 18th century origin. There was an evil look on the man's face. Newburgh's White Lady was unwelcome because she heralded imminent death.

A celebrated female ghost seen at North Kilvington near Thirsk was clad in white. The district belonged to the Meynells, followers of Norman William, who fought for him at Hastings. The name was inscribed on the scroll of Battle Abbey. Meynells remained staunch Catholics through the religious upsets and they took part in the Pilgrimage of Grace. Roger Meynell, of Kilvington Hall, had his property seized and forfeited after defying the king's men.

Roger fled but left a 17-year-old daughter in the house. When the commissioners arrived she was praying in the chapel; they dragged her from the altar, killed her and threw the body into a stream. Henceforth the White Lass was seen at Borrowby Bridge, an arrow-shot from the old Meynell Hall, which is now just a moated site. Mr. Consett of Brawith paid a Roman Catholic priest to exorcise the restless spirit annually for £2 a time, but he was not successful. The White Lass appeared near the bridge as recently as 1950. A witness early this century saw her walk into the water and not reappear.

When Fountains Hall, near Ripon, was built, stones from the Cistercian abbey were used. The hall, completed in 1611, is a remarkably fine example

**Fountains Abbey, near Ripon**

of a Jacobean dwelling. The daughter of Sir Stephen Vyner was 'cruelly done to death.' It may have been her ghost which was seen in the building, where she became known as the Blue Lady. Fountains Abbey ghosts have been filmed, in black and white and colour, when the abbey was floodlit, but the effects may be simply tricks of the light. A monochrome film recorded what were taken to be the faces of a monk and a girl on a pillar; the colour film picked up a strange shape on the building at night.

Ripon had an official called a Wakeman who was charged with the protection of the city at night. The last Wakeman, Hugh Ripley, became the first Lord Mayor in 1604. His house, which is partly of the 13th century, stands in the market place. Each evening a hornblower blows four blasts at the market cross and three at the residence of the Mayor. In 1923 the Mayor, who had married into the Precious family, one-time residents at the Wakeman's house, successfully urged the corporation to buy the building and preserve it. He asked that the horn should be blown here in addition to the other places, and this was agreed.

Did the ghost of Hugh Ripley find the idea attractive? The Mayor later reported: 'As soon as the first blast from the horn had been blown someone in the crowd called out "Look at the top window." As we looked, something white, with no distinguishable form, seemed to appear at the small window at the top. Whatever it might have been, everyone in the crowd saw this weird apparition at the window. People said it was the ghost of Hugh Ripley, aroused by the revival of the old custom outside his house. Those who were close by say that the "spirit" wore a ghostly smile at the honour paid by such a ceremony.'

The Precious family, who lived at the house for nearly a century until 1911, knew there was a ghost here. They had been awakened at night by a sense of a strange presence. Ghostly footsteps were heard. Chairs placed in the line taken by the ghost were pushed away during the night, and once a ghostly form was seen moving through a bedroom.

The ghost of Guy Fawkes is said to stalk the corridors of Scotton Old Hall, near Knaresborough. Slow and heavy footsteps have been heard along an upstairs passage at the *Royal Oak* in the town. At North Deighton Manor, near Wetherby, slow dragging footsteps were heard in a corridor.

Burton Agnes Hall, near Bridlington, was built by Sir Henry Griffith, who had three daughters. The youngest one, Anne, had delightedly watched the building progress at every stage until its completion in 1628. Anne visited the St. Quentins of Harpham Hall, about a mile away, returning in the evening with her dog. It was a period when robbers were active. There had been uneasy times since the dissolution of the monasteries and the rascals were called Wold Rangers. Some men asked Anne for alms, and as she drew off a glove to open her purse she incidentally revealed a valuable ring. One of the men struck her with a cudgel and stole the ring.

Anne died five days later from her injuries. In her last moments she implored her sisters to preserve her head in the new hall. They promised to do this, but the wish was not carried out. Anne was buried in Burton Agnes church. Loud crashes and groans and the slamming of doors disturbed the peace of Burton Agnes Hall. Female servants left. The distracted sisters asked Sir William St. Quentin, the vicar, what they must do. Eventually the coffin was opened and the body found intact except for the head, which was already a grinning skull.

The head was carried into the Hall, and peace followed, except on two occasions when the head was removed from the building. A servant girl threw it from a window on to a pile of manure in a passing cart; the horses stopped and would not move until the servant retrieved the skull. Then a member of the Boynton family, who had married a Strickland daughter, and now owned the Hall, buried the skull in the garden. There was an endless moaning, wailing and crying until it was restored. The skull was first kept on a table in the great saloon, but it was later bricked up in a wall.

Burton Constable, one of Yorkshire's stateliest halls, is said to be haunted by William Constable, a 19th century resident, who has been seen in the gold bedroom; his clothing included a quaint coat of velvet.

The imaginative quivered with fright when passing Gunnerside Lodge, Upper Swaledale, on stormy nights. Here might be seen a lady wearing a black dress, the ghost of a person who perished by fire.

# 3. Haunted Highways

TODAY, as we motor swiftly on good roads through the wilder parts of Yorkshire, we can have little understanding of the arduous and protracted journeys made by travellers on foot or horseback, or the terror they would feel when, in wild or gloomy weather, the inexplicable occurred.

If you see an elderly lady while motoring on the road between Aysgarth and Woodhall, do not offer her a lift. It is possibly a ghost. You can determine this exactly by reference to her clothes. The apparition is clad in black mid-Victorian dress and wears a coloured hat and white gloves. She carries a walking stick. The Black Lady has shown herself in recent times; she was seen at about 2 a.m. on a March morning in 1934, dressed in a fashion resembling the crinoline period.

It could be the same ghost as the woman in black observed walking from Coverham church gates to a point known as 'Curting Wall Corner', which is half way over Middleham Low Moor. This lady reputedly had two lovers. She made arrangements to run away with one of them, but the other found out and murdered her just before the elopement could take place. Three ladies from Tupgill about two miles from Middleham, saw a woman in black near a gate as they drove home in a trap. They asked the woman to open the gate. The lady unhelpfully vanished. Peat-cutters on Scrafton Moor early this century found the skeleton of a woman and the peat had preserved a fragment of black cloth.

A 'ghost light' reported from Coverdale may be related to a ruined chapel called St. Simons that stands between the hamlets of Caldeburgh and West Scrafton. The light appeared as a bright beam; motorists drew into the side of the road thinking that another vehicle was approaching.

Small cars could once be driven over the packhorse bridge at Knight Stainforth, in North Ribblesdale. No motorists reported seeing two ghosts, man and dog, who walked between the Hall and Dog Hill, but pedestrians have reported 'summat odd'. Historically the ghosts were connected with a part of Knight Stainforth Hall which was gutted by fire 200 years ago.

Ghosts usually instil fear into others. One Ribblesdale spectre is herself scared. The name Beggar's Wife Bridge, near Settle, relates to a beggar who went berserk and slew his wife. A witness described the ghost as 'a rushing shape with nothing but a cobweb for her face'. She looked fearfully behind her as though the beggar was still in pursuit.

The *White House* inn stood beside the Easingwold and Thirsk road. Three people who planned a murder here were hanged on gibbets at the roadside between Raskelf and Helperby, and three skulls were dug up about a century ago. The murdered man was an old Raskelf farmer called Thomas Fletcher. His ghost helped to bring the offenders to trial, and it also frequented the area for years afterwards. The coach horses reared and bucked at night as though sensing the supernatural.

Thomas Fletcher married his servant, Meg, but she returned to her former lover, Ralph Renard, who kept the inn. They decided to murder Fletcher, whose ostler agreed to keep them informed of the farmer's movements. On New Year's Day, as Fletcher returned home after visiting Topcliffe, the ostler signalled to the others as he approached. They grabbed Fletcher and drowned him in a beck, burying his body in the garden of the *White House*. Mustard seeds were sown on the grave. The ostler explained to inquirers that his master had left the district, but people gossiped when Meg was frequently seen to visit the *White House*.

She and Renard planned to marry. Renard visited Topcliffe Fair to buy her a present, and he stayed at the *Angel,* where Fletcher spent his last night. Renard woke when a horse neighed and he looked out of his bedroom window to see a bright light at the stable door. Also visible was the figure of Thomas Fletcher. Renard was upset when he returned home. The meal his sister prepared included mustard from the seeds planted on the grave of Fletcher, whose head appeared from a bright light glowing in the chair opposite the murderer as he dined. Renard brokenly told his sister what had happened and she reported the murder to a magistrate. So justice was done.

Three revellers, returning from races at Boroughbridge by moonlight, saw ghosts at the crossroads near Norton. The apparitions were recognised as Abbas on a white steed. Abbas pointed to the ground with a sword and rode away. Later a stoat with a dead rabbit in its mouth crossed the road and stood in the place indicated by the ghost. An arrow from an unseen bow

struck the stoat in the heart; someone, somewhere, laughed and chattered. Each element in this macabre story represented a coming event.

The night's happenings were blamed on a witch named Liza Horngill. Owen Metcalfe, of Dishforth, urged a crowd to drag Liza from her home and duck her in the pond. Liza screamed vengeance on Metcalfe as she crawled from the water, and she promised that two people in particular would be sorry. Metcalfe's girl friend, Alice Appleton, broke with him because of the cruelty he showed to Liza. That night the barn owls — Gabriel's ratchets — howled and cried, which was taken to mean that someone had died. The body of Alice was found in the pond, and it was accepted that she had been depressed by her broken romance and taken her own life.

Someone remembered the ghostly happenings at the crossroads and asked Liza for an explanation. The rabbit was Alice, killed by the stoat before the crossroads were reached. The stoat died when an arrow pierced it, and the arrow was a stake. Liza said the villagers must tell Owen Metcalfe to take the stake meant for Alice (as a suicide, she would have it pushed through her heart). The stake had to be thrown into the air and caught three times. Metcalfe obliged, but when he caught it a third time a splinter lodged between the thumb and forefinger of his hand, causing great suffering and eventually tetanus. Before his jaws locked he confessed to drowning Alice in the pond.

So Alice was buried in consecrated ground; her place in a grave at the crossroads was taken by the body of Metcalfe. It was laid at the spot which Abbas had indicated many night before.

Ralph Thoresby, the Leeds antiquary, passed Busby Stoop beside the Thirsk–Ripon road, in May, 1703, and saw the 'doleful object of Thomas Busby, hanging in chains for the murder of his father-in-law, Daniel Auty'. Maybe the antiquary came a little too soon after the event to hear about Busby's shadow, which haunted the area for a while. Auty, of Danoty Hall, was rich because of illegal activities, which included coining. His daughter married Thomas Busby and one night the men quarrelled. Auty, first reported missing, was later found to have been murdered. Busby was convicted. His body dangled from a gibbet at the crossroads.

A Scottish pedlar who visited Wetherby sold his wares at Clapgate and was not seen again — until a labourer, returning home on a lonely lane months later, saw the ghost of the man. The distraught look on the ghost's face was understandable, for the throat was cut from ear to ear. Men called the area Cut-Throat Hill. A ploughman working near the lane unearthed a skeleton buried head downwards with the spinal chord severed. It was decently reburied and the ghost of the little pedlar was not seen again.

Early this century, a traveller from Bridlington to Hornsea descended the brow of a hill to the south of Skipsea and saw a young woman dressed in white. She walked a little ahead of him and he followed her down the hill at a distance of 20 or 30 yards. The traveller expected she would turn here and cross the bridge. She approached the brook and then vanished 'at the very time my eyes were fixed on her'.

A farm servant went from Skipsea to Bridlington two hours before dawn.

He returned home in the afternoon before it was dark, reporting : 'As I cantered along Skipsea lane in the morning, bending forward with my face downward, the horse bolted from the road to such a distance that I was very nearly dismounted. On recovering myself and looking about, I saw a fine lady dressed in white, with something like a black veil over her head, standing close by. How I got to Skipsea I cannot tell, but I was so frightened I durst go no further, but I walked up and down the hill till it was light, when I found some persons going the same road, whom I accompanied to Bridlington.'

A spectral coach drawn by six horses has been seen racing down a fellside in upper Wensleydale. Ghostly coaches and four have been reported from near Stokesley and also near Brunton House, on the old road between Settle and Cross Streets, in North Craven. An urban happening was the presence of a ghostly coach and four at Beverley. The driver was reputedly Sir Josceline Percy (who died when he was poisoned by ungrateful servants in 1532). He was a well-connected man, being the son of the 4th Earl of Northumberland. Some accounts of the haunting refer to black horses without heads and the presence in the coach of a single passenger, a skeleton!

# 4. On the Moors

A FARMER'S daughter living near Horton, Bradford, became known as 'Fair Rebecca of Bradford-dale'. Her young man, who lived at Bracken Hall, 'betrayed' her on the promise of marriage. The story of Fair Rebecca was told in rather tedious verse; she dreamed on the day before her wedding should have taken place that she was dead and her head lay in a pool of blood. The dream came true. When the farm lad invited her to walk over the moors she accepted and he pushed her into a disused pit. Screams were heard from the pit after dark on stormy nights, and her ghost dressed in white appeared on the moor and occasionally at the village green.

Cliffs at the edge of the Hambleton Hills, in North Yorkshire, might have been fashioned for tragedy. In the reign of James I, men pursued a witch, Abigail Carstair, who dashed across the moors. She evaded her enemies but not death when she leapt from the crags of Whitestone Cliff. Was it Abigail's ghost who travelled between the crags and Gormire, a lake which has no conspicuous inflow or outflow?

A racecourse was once laid out on the Hambletons and here was seen a spectral horseman. The apparition of a white monk appeared about the cliff to warn travellers that there was a sheer drop ahead. The ghosts of horses are associated with some treacherous areas of bogland.

Boltby Bank, on an ancient way from Bilsdale to Thirsk, was haunted by a figure in black. A Durham solicitor, riding from Bilsdale on a summer day, stopped his horse to admire the view as he descended Boltby Bank. He felt inexplicably lonely, aching for someone with whom he could talk. A figure in black was walking down the bank ahead of him, but as he drew close to the figure — that of a tall, slim lady — she moved to a walled enclosure and vanished among the trees beyond a wall. The solicitor was told that a hall stood where the lady in black had vanished. The owner of the hall had murdered his wife and fled to France.

Sir Ernest Bennett, an enthusiastic collector of ghost stories, told of a haunting on Marston Moor, the scene of a battle of the Civil Wars fought — and won — by Cromwell's men in 1644. A commercial traveller who lived at Ripon drove a friend from Scarborough to Harrogate in November 1932. They crossed the farmlands of modern Marston Moor in poor visibility. The Ripon man slowed down when he saw a motor bus approaching and the driver of the bus reported men on the road. Though it was misty, the Ripon motorist and his friend saw three men wearing long, dark cloaks with dark-topped boots or leggings. They had large hats, turned up at the sides with cockades, and wore their hair long. The headlights on the car had been dimmed. When the Ripon man turned them to full power again on passing the bus, the mystery men were no longer visible. Were they the ghosts of men slain in the battle?

Does a ghostly army march through the area of the Forest of Knaresborough? Three farmers last century saw men clad in white and led by a commander who had a tunic of scarlet. Swords flashed in the sunlight. The farmers gravely assured their friends that they saw the apparitions well outside normal licensing hours.

# 5. Haunted Churches

THE most famous and best-documented of the Yorkshire ghosts is that of an Augustinian canon who has appeared fairly often at the Bolton Priory, in Wharfedale. A note about the sighting of the ghost in 1912 was included in Lord Halifax's *Ghost Book,* published in 1936. Some distinguished people guaranteed the correctness of the circumstances; they were King George V, the Duke of Devonshire, his son (the Marquis of Hartington) and Lord Desborough.

The Marquis, then a boy on vacation from Eton, and up at Bolton — as were others — for the grouse shooting, had been accommodated at the Rectory, which is believed to stand on the site of the Priory guest house. He went to his bedroom at 11-15 p.m. on August 18 and saw a figure standing at the door. The apparition was 'dressed in nondescript clothes and was more or less clean-shaven. I was at the top of the staircase, looking down the passage in which mine was the end room. I went downstairs again and fetched another light, but on going up again the figure had disappeared.' The ghost had been discussed that evening but the Marquis was not present at the talk; he later said that he was not thinking about a ghost when he went upstairs.

Further information was given to Lord Halifax by the Duchess of Devonshire, who quizzed her son carefully. 'He seems to be the same man who was seen two or three times by the Vicar, but the Vicar's ghost wore a brown dress and Eddy declares this man's was dark grey or black. Eddy's ghost had a round face — no beard, but what he described as a rough face. When we asked the Vicar afterwards if his ghost had a beard he said "No," but that he looked as if he had not shaved for four or five days, and his face was very round.' Incidentally, a Rector (not a Vicar) has the spiritual oversight at Bolton.

In his last point the Marquis was wrong. White (or undyed wool) was the raiment of the Cistercians, whose nearest important settlement was Fountains Abbey, near Ripon. The Augustinians were known as 'black canons'. A more recent sighting of the ghost disclosed the clothing was a black cassock-like robe with a woollen white overlay, black cloak, flat black hat. Augustinian canons were not subject to tonsure (the stylised clipping of the hair on the head) and were allowed to grow beards if they wished.

At the time when Lord Halifax's *Ghost Book* was published, the Rector of Bolton Abbey was the Rev. C. F. Tomlinson, who had become the incumbent a few years after the 1912 sighting. He did not hear or see anything inexplicable at the Rectory. Mr. Tomlinson's predecessor, the

Rev. James MacNabb, was standing by the window of an empty room in 1911 when he felt compelled to turn. As he spun round he saw the apparition in the doorway. The Rector moved and instantly the monk disappeared. A former agent of the estate, Mr. A. Downs, recalled in 1936 that Lord Charles Cavendish mentioned seeing the ghost about 1920. Another shred of evidence was offered by Mrs. Etchells, of Bolton Bridge Cottages. She was the daughter of a former blacksmith at Bolton. About 1896 when she was a child, her playmates spoke of a ghost at the Rectory, and they called it Punch.

**At Bolton Abbey**

So to the present day. A man entered the gatehouse in 1965 and saw the ghost walking towards him. A visitor saw the figure in the old choir. Virtually all recent sightings have been during July. Footsteps have been heard in parts of the Rectory. A Rector was sawing wood in the cellar of the old building when he heard the slap, slap of sandalled feet. They were moving across the floor above him; yet he was able to confirm he was alone in the house.

In spring, 1973, amateur archaeologists called off their search in Bolton Priory for the burial place of John de Clifford — 'The Butcher' — who was slain in the Wars of the Roses, 1461. During the search, a woman member of the team was confronted by a man in medieval costume. Another spoke of a vision of something 'very black and very evil' at the mouth of a tomb they had been excavating.

In a grave they excavated in the south transept of the ruins they found a woman's skeleton. They re-sealed the tomb and the strange experiences ceased. A team member, entering the church alone, had to leave because he felt something 'strong and very frightening'.

Many of the ghost stories of Yorkshire are silly or improbable but the monk of Bolton Priory — seen and reported on by several people up to modern times — is an apparition worthy of serious study. The angelus was heard at Bolton long after the bells had been removed. Among the men who claimed to have heard it was a former Archbishop of York.

Go to the churchyard at Kirkby Malham at midnight and you may find that a banquet has been spread out for you — by the Devil. This happens on 'a certain night' which is not specified. The story of Malhamdale's 'ban-quet of the dead' was first told in 1857, and it was re-told by J. H. Dixon. The Devil asked a boy named Kitchen and the Vicar (Rev. Martin Knowles) to his banquet, which was laid out on a tombstone. The Devil pronounced grace and chose 'De Profundis', remarking to the parson, 'Is not a "De Profundis" the most fitting one for the banquet of the dead?' The parson looked over the range of food and asked for salt. All the food — and the Devil — disappeared. If you take up an invitation to a midnight feast in the churchyard do not ask for salt, and remember that once you go to the banquet you will 'go always and finally sup with the old gentleman in his abode of darkness'.

The apparition of a monk has been reported from St. Michael's church, Linton, which has a solitary, riverside setting in Upper Wharfedale.

The Abbey House at Kirkstall, Leeds, has a monastic background where ghosts will presumably feel at home. A woman who looked after the building for nine years until 1935 saw only one ghost — an abbot — pacing the building. That was all, apart from strange noises sometimes heard at night which she thought were made by birds entering chinks in the wall.

A ghost at Whitkirk was heard but not seen in the corridors of the vicarage, a Georgian house built on to part of a 17th century farmhouse. Heavy footsteps like those made by a man walking on stone flags were heard, yet the corridors were carpeted. A Whitkirk vicar and two friends saw a spectral dog moving across the garden.

Guisborough, in Cleveland, records a figure in white sitting on a tomb-stone. The tower at Rievaulx Abbey, near Helmsley, has been bare for centuries but bells are sometimes heard at night. A guest staying at a big house in the district 40 years ago came down to breakfast and complained that he had been kept awake by church bells. The story acquired a fanciful touch when it was reported that the bells played a definite tune; the score was sent to the British Museum where an expert said it was a tune likely to have been used when Rievaulx Abbey was occupied by monks.

Wass, which lies beside a road that has descended from the moors close to Byland Abbey, has the story of a shepherd who walked in the fields on Christmas Eve about 1850. The night was moonlit and he could look down on the remains of Byland Abbey. He saw a monk moving among the ruins and also heard the Magnificat being sung by an unseen choir.

Only one ghost of any fame has haunted the Minster in York. Dean Gales was such a well-known ghost in his time that the diarist Samuel Pepys asked about him. Gale had a great affection for the Minster. He died within its precincts in 1702 and a week later he was buried within the building in a coffin of lead.

The last Abbess of a convent attached to Holy Trinity Church in Micklegate, York, was a heroine. Soldiers arrived to carry out Henry VIII's commands about dissolution and she defied them. They would enter the place only over her dead body; if she died she would haunt the place until another sacred building rose on the spot. The soldiers slew her and her ghost returned, first to the convent, then — with its demolition — to Holy Trinity Church. The Abbess was most often seen on Trinity Sunday, sometimes in the company of another woman and a child.

Clementhorpe is now a populous area of York. Before it was developed it was visited at night by the ghost of Archbishop Scrope, who had been beheaded at the command of Henry IV in 1405 following a travesty of a trial at Bishopthorpe. The execution took place in a field at Clementhorpe, and here the prelate was first interred, the body being subsequently moved to the Minster. Travellers saw a coffin covered with a black pall fringed with white silk slowly floating through the air. Behind the coffin walked a robed Archbishop who read quietly from an open book, though no sound came from his moving lips. Why should the Archbishop conduct his own funeral service? How was his head restored to his shoulders? It is now impossible to locate the exact site of execution.

Canon J. Solloway told a ghost story about Selby in 1936. A curate was alone in the abbey after evening service. As he removed vestments in the sacristy he heard a voice, followed by what sounded like groans. The curate went to the sacristy door and called to ask who was in pain. More groans were heard. The curate dashed to Canon Solloway, who felt like reproving him because an opportunity to have an insight into the spirit world might have been missed. 'The old monks would have given anything for a chance like that,' he said. 'Didn't you feel inclined to look more closely into the matter?' The curate, with simple candour: 'No sir, I ran like the devil!'

The ghost of Abbess Hilda is said to haunt the remains of her abbey at Whitby. Watton Priory between Driffield and Beverley, was possibly a nunnery in its earliest days. Danish invaders sacked the place in the 9th century and it was refounded by Lord Eustace Fitz-John of Knaresborough in the 12th century at the instigation of Henry Murdac, Archbishop of York. The Archbishop visited Watton twice in a vision, or so a fanciful story relates. Murdac placed a four-year-old girl, Elfrida, at Watton and it was intended that she would take the veil. Elfrida grew into a good-looking woman, which made the Sisters jealous and diverted the attention of the lay brethren who managed the secular affairs.

Elfrida and one of the brothers met secretly. She, an honest lass, confessed her fault to her Superiors and asked to leave the community. This could not be allowed because of the scandal. Instead she was stripped, stretched on the floor, scourged with rods, cast in a dungeon without light, fettered by iron chains to the floor and given only bread and water, 'which was administered with bitter taunts and reproaches'.

Elfrida saw the Archbishop in a vision, and he told the girl that she had cursed him and urged her to repent. She must recite certain psalms as well. Apart from her injuries, Elfrida was in an 'interesting condition'. What should be done with the infant? The Archbishop appeared in a vision and, assisted by two women, delivered the child. In the morning Elfrida was found in good health, clear of her fetters and standing free. Ailred, Abbot of Rievaulx, was asked to study the case and he pronounced it a miracle.

Here the story ends, but Watton was haunted by a headless nun. It is unlikely to have been Elfrida and could have been the ghost of a woman beheaded in the 17th century. Watton ladies were ill-fated. During the Civil Wars a band of Puritan soldiers stormed across the Wolds. The owner of Watton was a staunch Royalist who was fighting for the King many miles away. His wife, left with only a few servants for protection, took her child and valuables to a wainscot room from which there was a secret exit from the house.

The soldiers found the other end of the secret way as they poked about the area of the moat. Ascending the stairs they broke down a panel leading into the room. The child was dashed against a wall and killed. Her ladyship was struck down and beheaded. The house was plundered.

St. Mary's churchyard, in Scarborough, is an excellent place for ghost-hunting. A moving shadow has been seen near the remains of the abbey's great east window. On St. Mark's Eve (April 24) the forms of those who will die within the next year form a sad little procession which goes into the church. It is unlucky to fall asleep if you decide on a St. Mark's vigil; sleep means certain death within the year. A Scarborough woman went to St. Mary's on that evening in 1786 and she recognised herself in the line of forms passing by. In effect she saw her own ghost, and collapsed and died. Modern sceptics wonder how she managed to tell of her experiences.

# 6. Spectral Hounds

THE spectral dog has been seen throughout England and also in Continental Europe. Two types are known — the Barguest (also called Padfoot and Guytrash) and the Black Dog. Barguest has taken other forms, including those of bear and sheep. It portends doom. The Black Dog, usually (though not always) very dark, is less frightening than the Barguest. It has been known to be well-disposed towards people.

Few tracks in the Dales are better known than the Corpse Way, in Swaledale. The bodies of daleheaders were carried along it for about 12 miles to the nearest consecrated ground, Grinton. The lane crosses the Swale by a hump-backed bridge at Ivelet. Incidentally, a coffin-sized stone almost buried at the roadside on the northern side is called 'coffin stone' without cause. It was probably placed here to reinforce the bridge. Edmund Cooper has written: 'It may be argued that it owes its name not to the use made of it, but to its striking likeness to the shape of a coffin.' One might expect a human ghost in this area, but the local apparition is a black dog, which is seen running on to the bridge and then falling from a ledge. The dog is said to herald a tragic event. Yet this animal was last reported a century and more ago. Some of the lead minders, returning home with 'skinfuls of ale', were an easy prey for local superstitions.

What is believed to be the Barguest lay up in Trollers Gill but haunted a wider area. It was reported to be about the size of a small donkey, black and shaggy, with eyes as big as saucers. An eyewitness noticed its immense eyes and added that the beast was 'big as a littleish bear, and yellow'! Ghostly situations can easily be fabricated. Fred Cobley, in his book *On the Foot in Wharfedale,* wrote entertainingly of a Threshfield man who had a large billy goat. The wags of the village sometimes put a chain round its neck and let it wander along the lanes at night. Farmers returning home from Kettlewell market quivered with fear as they saw or heard the goat.

A miller drove by in a horse-drawn cart at about 10 p.m. one market day and the goat was wandering about. The chain round its neck rattled loudly. Thinking of the Barguest, the miller knelt in the bottom of his cart and, to the amusement of the lads concealed behind a wall, prayed fervently for deliverance from the hound. He promised not to cheat again over the sale of his meal.

The Barguest was reported from the moors above Ilkley and Otley. In pre-gaslight days, thoughts of the Guytrash upset imaginative people at Skipton. The Rev. S. Baring Gould, who was at Horbury in the 1860s, wrote that the Padfoot was said to haunt a lane near Ossett, 'to the terror of the mill-girls'.

The Washburn Valley had a spectral dog that talked — in 'broad Yorkshire'! An improbable Victorian record relating to Dob Park Lodge now ruined, tells of a man who located a passage leading into a brightly-lit room. Here stood a padlocked chest and a two-handed sword. On the lid of the chest was a glass containing a golden fluid. The guardian of the room was a large black mastiff, with eyes as big as saucers and 'bright as fire'. It rose as the man entered the room and said 'Now tha's come, lad, tha mun either sup yon cup, or draw yon sword, or open yon kist.' The visitor drank from the cup. Then the sword drew itself and the chest began to open. The golden draught burnt his tongue like liquid fire and he coughed and spluttered. A clap of thunder was heard, the mastiff howled and all the lights went out. When the man stumbled from the cavern his hair had gone white!

Ghostly dogs — this time doubtless a benevolent variant of the Black Dog — helped devout folk. A Congregational minister was assisted at a moment of danger while travelling from Wigglesworth to Tosside. In the Aire Valley, a Methodist named Thomas Jackson Reynard walked from Keighley to Silsden late one February day in 1893. A little way out of Keighley he had to pass through a wood. When he was almost under tree-cover he felt something touch his leg. It was a large collie dog, which followed him, keeping close to his heels. Mr. Reynard saw two men at the roadside ahead; as he passed them the dog took up a position in between. At his Silsden home his wife was worried about him. A neighbouring farmer, knowing that Mr. Reynard was walking from Keighley, called to see if he had returned home safely. The farmer's son had been attacked and injured on that road by two men who took his watch and money.

A phantom dog has also been seen at Colton, near Leeds. A ghost story of a dog-that-never-was has been told of an unnamed old house 'on the cliffs not far from Whitby'. The premises had been converted into a nursing home. A new member of the staff who was led into a room that was small and well-panelled was warned that a ghost had already caused two nurses to leave. As they slept they felt suffocated, as though a dog lay on their chests. The ghost story had the backing of historical fact, for over a century before a girl was found murdered and her black collie dog lay across her body on the day following, refusing to leave or take food and drink. The dog died on the day she was buried. Was the faithful dog creeping into the bedroom each night to lie on the sleeper?

The new member of the staff awoke on two successive nights with the feeling of suffocation and insisted that a thorough search should be made. A hitherto unknown passage was located and it led the investigators by steps to a cave at the foot of the cliff. A grilled ventilator had been fitted to the foot of a panel giving access to the passage. As the cave filled with the flow tide each night, air was forced up the passage and it slightly compressed in the bedroom. The bedroom was provided with extra ventilation and the 'ghost dog' did not trouble the sleeper again.

Spectral dogs were reported from Kirkby Overblow, Cowling and Haworth. At Kirkby Overblow a farmer left his dog guarding sheep and forgot about it. The dog wandered home during the night and scratched on the door, but no one attended to it. The animal cleared off and starved to death; later a phantom dog was reported in the district. Explanations were possible. A man walking on the north side of the upper Swale at night, heard the rattling of a chain; he tremblingly went to investigate and came across a stray dog that had been dragging a chain. It had become entangled with a gate.

The white hare seen running on the cliff near Scarborough has been associated with the tragic death of a maid at nearby Cloughton Hall; this event took place last century.

# 7. Mysterious Castles

DOES the ghost of Lady Ann Day still haunt Barnard Castle, Teesdale, from which impressive fortress she fell to her death? Her ladyship lived in the reign of Queen Mary. She was flung from the castle walls into the Tees by an un-named enemy. In the occasional re-enactment of the tragedy, she moaned and lamented before taking a high dive from the battlements.

Bowes, near Barnard Castle, was visited by Charles Dickens when he was writing of terrible conditions at Dotheboys Hall. This village is no Victorian upstart, for the Roman road from York to Carlisle passed through, and one of the guardian forts lay at Bowes. What remains of a later castle can be visited by the public.

Bowes is haunted by a squad of ghosts. For the details, we must think of the twilight of the Roman Empire, and the recalling of legions from Britain to help with the defence of Rome. The garrison at Bowes ran amok and stole anything made of gold, presumably wanting worthwhile souvenirs of their stay in the North. Angry people attacked the fort and massacred the garrison just after the gold had been hidden, so none of it was recovered. It was said that on the anniversary of the massacre the ghosts of the murdered men appeared within the fort and went through the ritual of burying the gold.

Two men of the 17th century concealed themselves within the castle at Bowes on the anniversary night, seeing the spectral procession and a large chest, which was lowered into a vault at the north corner of the tower. This at least is the story — and it is a good story — but who related it? Both the Peeping Toms died violently. The first was slain by his friend, who then grovelled in the earth for the chest. A blood-red hand appeared, led the murderer over the body of his friend and across fields to the bank of the flooded Greta. Next day his body lay on the rocks there.

Did Thompson, a Richmond (Swaledale) potter, really see King Arthur and his Knights (plus the Round Table, horn and sword) in a vault deep under the castle? An old story claims this to be true. The story may first have been recounted by Breton soldiers who garrisoned Richmond Castle in Norman days. If men lie at rest in a deep vault, are they ghosts or men in that kind of suspended animation popularised by Rip Van Winkle? The potter was alone when he found the vault. He knew enough about such circumstances to attempt to draw the sword and blow the horn so that the treasure would be his. The eyes of the knights flickered and opened as he reached for the sword. The petrified potter fled and he could not find the vault again.

Arthur and his knights are said to sleep beneath Freeborough Hill in Cleveland.

At Skipsea, on the Yorkshire coast, a Flemish knight, a follower of William the Conqueror, was given land soon after the Conquest. He built a castle, of which a knoll called Albermarle Hill now remains. The knight, Drogode Bevere, earned Royal favour when he married William's niece, but he was excessively cruel to her and eventually surreptitiously gave her some poison. He asked the King's permission to visit the Continent so that he could show his wife the land of his birth, and before William discovered what had happened to his niece he had got beyond range. The Skipsea area was periodically haunted by a lady wearing white. The apparition appeared both during the night and in the day, sometimes with a head and at others without it!

Ghosts reported from Snape Castle, near Masham, quite possibly relate to the spirit of Katherine Parr, last wife of Henry VIII. The present owners have never seen her, but several independent witnesses have at various times this century seen the ghost of a young girl dressed in a blue Tudor-style dress, with long, fair hair showing around a small cap. This ghost is said to be friendly and happy, which consoles me. I once unsuspectingly slept in the haunted room!

Piers Gaveston haunts the keep of Scarborough Castle. Piers was beheaded at Warwick in 1312, but a short time before he had been holding out with his forces at Scarborough. He surrendered on condition that his life would be spared. He was too trusting. His enemies abducted him, and he was slain.

# 8. River Hauntings

SIR WALTER SCOTT, the novelist, enjoyed visiting Rokeby, where the Tees is joined by the Greta. His special local friend was John Morritt, the squire of Rokeby Hall, a home built by the Rokebys when their older residence was destroyed by Scottish raiders in the reign of Edward II. Morritt told Sir Walter about a headless lady who haunted Mortham Tower.

Centuries before, a Rokeby had married a most beautiful woman. He became insanely jealous, believing that she had become the mistress of a northern baron. He hacked off her head and dumped the remains into the Tees. On his return to Mortham Tower he saw that blood was dripping from his dagger. He tried unsuccessfully to wipe away the stains. The apparition was of a lady who trailed a length of white silk behind her.

Early in the 18th century a parson found the ghost under the river bridge and reported that he had conversed in Latin (quite how, in the absence of her head, is not recorded). The arch of the bridge was swept away in 1771. The headless lady has been seen in a bedroom at Mortham Tower within the last 20 years and, true to form, she was trailing a piece of white silk behind her.

Edward Garrett recorded that a monk 'visited' the river Tees at Egglestone Bridge. The spectre might have been connected with a chapel which stood on the bank in the days when travellers had to ford the river. The monk gave the impression that he had lost something; he was still reported to be looking around at his last appearance in 1928.

The mistress of Waddow Hall, near the Ribble, was reputedly a witch. She had a disagreement with a servant, Peg o' Nell, and sent her on a hazardous expedition to the river for water. It was hazardous because she cast a spell over her. The river banks and stepping-stones were sheathed with ice. The servant slipped and drowned. A spring near the river was called Peg o' Nell's Well and every seventh year — on Peg's Night — some creature (maybe a cat or dog) was drowned in the Ribble. If no animal perished, a human life was taken. One Peg's Night a young man and his horse were swept down the river and drowned.

As it flows between Barden and Bolton, the Wharfe is forced into a narrow channel between banks of gritstone that are so close together foolish visitors leap across, not always successfully. People who fall into the Strid are usually dragged into the depths and their bodies washed up on the banks lower down. Beware of a milk-white horse, for it is an omen of death. The horse usually appears on May Day prior to a death, and a fairy is also

**Cawood, on the Ouse. At this village was seen the ghost of Mary Barwick.**

reported to rise out of the Strid. Three sisters, heiresses of the Mauleverers of Beamsley, set out one May morning to watch for the white horse and to ask the fairy to grant them a wish. All three were found drowned. A donkey with brass eyes is said to frequent the Scroggs side of the river Swale near Ivelet.

One of the best-known Yorkshire river sprites is the ghost of Tom Hoggett, a highwayman arrested at the *Salutation Inn* on the Great North Road. He escaped from his captors and planned to cross the river by one of the two fords near Langton. The water was deeper than he expected and he was drowned at a place called Hoggett's Holme. Tom's ghost haunted the river, luring swimmers to their doom.

Murder at a pond forms the basis of a story told at Cawood, by the Ouse. William Barwick, like many before him, had married his girl friend because she was pregnant. He went for a walk with the former Mary Lofthouse near Cawood Castle in April 14, 1690, and pushed her into a pond, holding her under water until she had drowned. Hiding the body in some bushes, he returned next evening to bury her. Meanwhile he told his brother-in-law, Thomas Lofthouse, that his wife had gone to stay with her uncle at Selby. Lofthouse checked this story after seeing the ghost of Mary near the pond. At least, there was an apparition wearing a brown dress and white hood, similar to clothes worn by his sister. When it was found that Mary had not been to Selby a warrant was issued for Barwick's arrest.

He denied the charge of murder and said he sold his wife for five shillings. There was an idea current at the time that wife-selling was legal if certain simple formalities were observed. Barwick was tried, found guilty and put to death by being hanged in chains. When the body of Mary Barwick was given a Christian burial, her ghost did not walk again.

# 9. Tales from the Underworld

YORKSHIRE'S underworld of potholes, caves and man-made shafts and galleries was tailor-made for dwarfs, who often emerged from holes in the earth at night to threaten men. Solitary shepherds saw dwarfs at lambing time or just before a storm broke. An eyewitness described a creature as having bow legs and hollow eyes.

A tapping sound in a Swaledale lead mine was ascribed to 'wee folk' or to 't'awd man', as past generations of lead-miners were collectively known. Tapping in a mine — even a deserted mine — indicated that reserves of lead remained to be discovered. Modern explorers, moving with ultra-caution along old levels, find 'luck' or 'charm' stones, which have holes in the middle; they were hung up to ward off evil spirits. Superstitious miners (which meant virtually all miners) wore similar stones on strings around their necks.

Connected with the Lost Johns' system in High Craven is the story of a 'ghost that never was'. The name is plural; two Johns were involved and apparently found their way to the surface again. Swithinbank and Booth, members of the Yorkshire Ramblers' Club, saw a 'terrible' sight in a streamway leading to the final chamber. They were moving ahead of the main party and stopped for refreshments in the gloomy cave.

The passage became luminous; a soft glow gradually developed into a glowing mass of light which concentrated in the centre and took a vague shape. As the form approached it emitted a smell which the men recognised with considerable relief. Swithinbank had stuck a candle on the side of the passage to light up a space where tackle could be stacked well clear of the water. The men moved off a little way. The candle fell on to the tackle and fired the inflammable cover of a length of telephone wire, and so was created the ghost of Lost Johns'.

A boggart lived in Hurtle Pot, just behind St. Leonard's Church, Chapel-le-Dale, near Ingleton. He drowned people in the pool at the bottom — a pool which has for many years contained very dark-coloured trout. A courting couple walking near the hole fled when they heard weird strains coming from it. If they had waited they might have seen a musician emerge with a violin, on which he had been practising!

Fell Beck, rising high in Ingleborough, flows down the mountain's eastern side to where the water tumbles 340 feet into Gaping Gill, one of Britain's largest natural chambers. Potholers explore Gaping Gill, with its ramification of passages, by descending on ladders via Bar Pot and, much more rarely — because of the amount of equipment needed — make ladder descents down the main shaft. The Craven Pothole Club's *Journal* for 1964 tells of a ghost seen in Gaping Gill at a time when winch descents were being organised.

A potholer, named Fred in the piece, was the last in a queue to be drawn up by the bosun's chair. He looked on to a boulder slope and saw a light, suggesting that another potholer was below ground. Fred went up the slope to where the light was shining, but it was extinguished as he drew near. Using his own headlamp he picked out the form of a monk who had bent to lift a book from the slope. The apparition vanished. About this time potholers found human bones in Gaping Gill, and their presence was never satisfactorily explained.

Tom Greenwood, who was the manager of White Scar show cave, in Chapel-le-Dale, described a bird that he, his daughter and another person had seen underground on different occasions. It was not a bat, being much larger, dark blue in colour. The object flew with a gentle gliding movement, haunting the passage between the entrance of the cave and the first waterfall. In September, 1933, a Blackpool clairvoyant visited Mr. Greenwood and predicted that explorers in the cave system would reach sand in vast quantities and also find gold cups and ornaments. No gold has yet been found. A ring of gold, reputedly stolen by a deer-stalker, is said to lie at the bottom of Rowten Pot, Gragareth, above Kingsdale. The thief fled across the fells but tumbled into the open shaft. His body was found but the gold remains.

On the bank of the Ribble downriver from the packhorse bridge at Stainforth lies the unimpressive mouth of a natural shaft, Robin Hood's Mill, named after a miller who worked his stones on a Sunday. His premises sank into the ground, but the millstones continued to revolve. Potholers investigated the shaft in the 1930s and subtly altered its shape. The mysterious grinding sound was not heard again.

Supernatural beings tapped in the lead mines of Greenhow, between Wharfedale and Nidderdale. A miner who followed the sounds might locate the richest lodes. Few of the miners bothered about inquiring too closely into eerie tappings and a Yorkshire system known to be haunted was usually worked by two or more men. A haunted area like Gill Field Level, near Greenhow, was not for solo exploration. A bogle living in Clayshaw Level, Nidderdale, pushed the wagons about!

Mr. George Gill, who has managed the show caves at Stump Cross, Greenhow Hill, for many years, used to live at a cottage in the fell-top village. One moonlit night he heard the sound of clogs on the gravel of the road, then on the cobblestones by its side and finally on the gritstone slab by his front door. He and his wife looked out. There was no one to be seen. A member of a cave survey group camping at Stump Cross one moonlit night heard the sound of clogs on the road. The sounds passed him and went towards Greenhow. No one was in sight!

Three members of the Earby Mine Research Group were sitting in a drift at Buckden Gravel Mine, Upper Wharfedale, coiling up rope after exploration, when two members, who were close together, heard a voice suddenly and sharply call 'Hey!' The third member of the party heard nothing. The men assured themselves there was no one else in the system.

A building at Grinton Smelt Mill that served as a blacksmith's shop, with an office above, was used as overnight accommodation by two Earby mine researchers one snowy night. They transferred some equipment to the old office, then parked the car outside, leaving it in gear and locking the doors. One man, hearing an unusual sound during the night, went outside. The car was absent, but there were tracks in the snow (with the tread of tyres distinct). The car had run some short distance, turned off the track and gone down towards a stream. The men chocked the wheels. The doors were found to be locked and the gear lever still engaged.

Later in the night the men returned to the car. Tracks in the snow indicated that it had moved again — sideways! This time the car was secured to its position by stakes driven into the ground and 100 feet of rope. Next morning the vehicle had to be 'wound' back to the road in low gear using the starter handle. It was returned to the old office, parked and brakes released. It ran in the opposite direction to that taken the night before. (The office and blacksmith's shop have since been demolished.)

Ghosts in the coal mines of South Yorkshire had their peace shattered by modern high-speed machines slicing away the seams.

Workers in the Haigh Moor seam at Hemsworth were terrified early this century when eyes gleamed at them from the darkness. The points of light could have been fireflies introduced to the pit in foreign timber. A 'ghost' in a colliery near Barnsley tapped in an area where a tragic accident had occurred; the mine surveyor laid the ghost when he found that the tapping was water trickling to the floor from the roof of the old seam.

# 10. An Assortment of Ghosts

GOATHLAND, in a saucer-shaped green depression surrounded by heather, had a 'bogle-house' at Greenend. When it was demolished the ghost of a tailor's apprentice was homeless. The tailor — a typical country craftsman who spent much of his time going from farm to farm, meeting orders on the spot — was an obsessed card-player. He and his wife invited people to Greenend for card games and the hosts invariably came off best. The apprentice noticed that the couple were crafty cheats. He must have mentioned this to them and he was seen no more. The house acquired a ghost. A farmer who passed this way in the 1890s reported that fire darted from a garden drain!

The story, like much else at Goathland, is very old. So is the tale of a dead warrior whose spirit cried out from a pool at Water Ark and was put to rest by a Scottish visitor who played the pipes all the way from the pool to the churchyard. Goathland took its spirit world so seriously that a Watcher was appointed to peer into the future and to advise anyone who might be bewitched. By standing at the junction of the village road and the Beckhole road and staring hard towards Beckhole and the bottom of the dale he could tell how long it would be before a death occurred — also, indeed, with extra concentration, the names of those who would attend the funeral. The Goathland Watcher was 'always reet.'

The ghost of widow Kay, who died at Cleckheaton in 1831, haunted a farmhouse she had willed to a nephew. It took the efforts of three parsons to exorcise her.

Before wills were commonly used, a person reaching old age would divide up the money among relatives and friends. A wealthy woman died at Nessag Farm, Moorsome, on the North York Moors, before she had made her wishes known. There was no excuse for this for she had lived to an advanced age. Relatives almost tore the house to pieces looking for money and they then put the farm up for rent. One family after another came, spent a few weeks here and left, convinced that the place was haunted. Had the old lady returned?

A woman with strong nerves leased the house and she regularly saw the ghost of the lady in the kitchen. One day the ghost wafted a cushion from a chair as she passed it and the tenant helpfully replaced it. The ghost, delighted by her consideration, pointed to a stone in the floor near the fire. The stone was lifted (with the ghost as an excited spectator) and the money was found underneath. The ghost of the old lady was not seen again. Presumably her mission ended when the money was handed to a person who deserved it.

**Castle Bolton, Wensleydale, was re-visited by Betsy Horne**

The womenfolk of the fishing communities helped the men by gathering bait for lines. When Hannah Grundy, a Staithes girl, rested on the beach at the bottom of a steep cliff in 1807, she could not foresee that she would die in an instant and that her spirit would haunt the neighbourhood. A falling stone neatly sliced off her head. For some time afterwards a headless ghost was seen in the area.

At Stockton-on-the-Forest, four miles north-east of York, a large army, and some trees, were seen in the sky on January 13, 1792, by 'persons of credit'. The army moved 'in separate divisions, some in black and others in white uniforms of which appeared a number of fir trees, which seemed to move along with the line in different directions and sometimes with great rapidity.'

York's *Theatre Royal* may occupy a monastic site. At about 2.30 a.m. two women who were lodging near the theatre heard a few bars of organ music coming from the theatre. The strains were heard again later in the night. They asked about it next day, but the mysterious noises were never explained. It is an odd story, for it cannot be seriously suggested that a medieval monastry had an organ.

When Betsy Horne of Castle Bolton died in 1944 everyone was sad, for she was well liked. On the night after she died George Jackson was writing in his cottage shortly after midnight when the door opened and Betsy entered. She was wearing her grave clothes and carried some roses. Mr. Jackson heard that Betsy visited another house in the village that night; she also appeared in a house at Leyburn.

A headless ghost seen at Rigg House, near Hardraw, Wensleydale, was believed to be of an old woman who worked as a housekeeper for a man called Metcalfe. He was not very well liked in the dale, possibly because he was a slave owner before settling here. Did he murder his housekeeper? Metcalfe left the valley and the ghost persisted in haunting a room at Rigg House until that part of the building was demolished.

The Rev. Robert Thomlinson, Master of Skipton Grammar School, was believed to have been frightened to death by the ghost of his predecessor, the Rev. Thomas Gartam, who had died ten years earlier after an unsuccessful three-years' struggle on Thomlinson's part to have him dismissed.

The ghost of Sir Henry Irving was said to haunt the *Theatre Royal,* Manningham Lane, Bradford, where he played his last role. It was after Sir Henry played the title role in *Becket* in October, 1905, that he collapsed and died in the foyer of the *Midland Hotel.*

Beverley has been well provided with ghosts. A death coach with four black horses issued from Gilby's Yard and went to St. Mary's church in North Bar Street. The driver and also the passengers inside were skeletons. Any person seeing this gruesome spectacle would die within the year.

Behind this tradition is a story that one of the Gilbys murdered his valet, named Jocelin, and buried him in a midden in the grounds, thinking to hide his crime. Jocelin's ghost made the lives of the family so miserable that the services of the Vicar were requisitioned to lay the ghost, which stipulated that it would remain quiet for 1,000 years. To this the Vicar agreed. There was a closet in the room in which the valet had been murdered and a thousand nails were driven into the door. One nail, it was said, flew out each year on the anniversary of the laying of the ghost. One of the Gilbys, with a view to improving the appearance of the grounds, ordered the midden to be emptied and its contents taken to a field at Norwood. When the cart with its contents reached St. Mary's burial ground, the horses refused to go any farther. The cart tipped up and out rolled a skull. It was buried in the place from which it had been taken. Peace was restored.

A skull kept at Browsholme Hall, in Bowland, is not ghostly in itself but strange events occurred when it was taken from the building. The hall was built over 400 years ago by the Parkers, who took their name from their historic occupation — park-keepers in the Forest of Bowland. The skull, kept in a court cupboard in the Tudor hall, is believed to have been from a martyr of the Pilgrimage of Grace and may have been kept originally in a chapel on the top storey of the house; this storey was removed in 1703. Edward Parker, on vacation from Harrow in the late 1850s, buried the skull in the garden as a joke, starting a chain reaction of strange happenings. The face of the hall crumbled and left the Tudor walls; beams smouldered and fired; an unusually large number of deaths occurred in the family. Edward

admitted removing the skull, which was returned to the house. The disasters stopped but for a while the family had to leave the hall while it was being renovated.

Sounds, not sightings, characterised the ghost of Low Hall, Appletreewick, a ghost which was eventually laid in Dib Gill. B. J. Harker, in *Rambles in Upper Wharfedale* (1869), reported that the building was often disturbed by unearthly sounds. The 'old shining pewter in the oaken case was rattled by the invisible being until it seemed as though the whole of it would be brought to the floor; the doors of the rooms were often banged open with terrible force and the rafters creaked and groaned.'

Golfers using Woodsome Hall, near Almondbury, may smile when they see a robin. Woodsome was occupied by the Kays, and their steward, Mr. Rimmington, died in 1697. His ghost returned from time to time. Hobkirk, in *Huddersfield, its History and Natural History,* reported that strange noises were heard in a room of the hall called 'Rimmington's closet.' A man met the ghost as it rode a horse at great speed down Woodsome Lane with a couple of dogs (presumably also spectral) on a leash. The galloping ghost plucked a brag-nail from a door post at the bottom of Farnley village. Local clergy put the unquiet spirit to rest, laying it in a small bathroom, but the ghost of Mr. Rimmington was metamorphosed into a robin (robinet) which visited the bathroom regularly. Farnley people were called robinets after this bird.

A coachman on the York-Hull run features in a story from Sheriff Hutton. Two centuries and more ago, Nance was the belle of the village. She deserted her boy friend Tom for a gay young blood from London. He was faithless and a year later Nance wandered wearily back towards her old home with a small child. Tom, originally a farm man and now a coachman, picked up Nance and her offspring as she stood ill and forlorn at the roadside. Nance died in Tom's arms. In a last exchange of words Tom offered to look after the child and Nance vowed, in turn, to watch over coach-drivers. Two years later Tom drove a special coach, engaged by four notables (incuding a bishop and a duke) from Durham to York. It was important to his clients that he should reach York quickly. Ten miles from the city the coach ran into fog, which thickened as the journey continued. A slight figure — it could only be the ghost of Nance — appeared on the box beside Tom and she took hold of the reins. Nance guided them safely and quickly to York.

Charlotte Brontë wrote: 'Speak of the North — a lonely moor silent and still and trackless lies . . .' Charlotte has not been seen in ghostly form, but her Haworth moors have their strange stories, including that of a ghost supposed to have haunted the old *Sun Inn* for many years. The interior of the inn was renovated and re-opened in 1792. The landlord heard about the ghost from the villagers, but did not believe in it. Yet he had a carved stone-head erected over the entrance porch, following local tradition that these were put on buildings when a workman had been killed on the site before it was completed. They are supposed to ward off evil spirits.

The spirit of Sister Hylda roamed the gentler, more fertile Arthington district in mid-Wharfedale over 700 years ago. She appeared in houses, glared at labourers in the fields and even floated over men's heads as she crossed the river. After seven years of the haunting, the Lady Abbess of Nun Appleton went into action in 1200. She called the Archbishop from Cawood,

nuns from St. Mary's (York) and the nuns of Arthington. High mass was chanted on the eve of St. Mark's day and the wandering spirit was laid to rest. Sister Hylda had become a pitiful sight, wounded in the breast and with sunken eyes from which incessant tears rained. She appeared during Mass with Friar John, whom Hylda accused of dishonouring and murdering her. He, stricken with remorse, had made pilgrimages to many shrines. No more was seen of them. The nunnery at Arthington went long ago, but the name was perpetuated by a house dating from the reign of Charles I.

A worshipper at Holy Trinity church, York, in 1876 had been staring at 'the left or north side of the window' when he saw a 'bright light, formed like a female, robed and hooded, passing from north to south with a rapid gliding motion outside the church, apparently at some distance. There are four divisions in the window, all of stained glass, but at the edge of each runs a rim about two inches wide, and joining the stonework. Through the rim especially could be seen what looked like a form transparent, but yet thick with light . . . About half an hour later it again passed from north to south, and having remained about 10 seconds only returned with what I believe to have been the figure of a young child. It stopped at the last pane but one and vanished.' The child was not seen again, but the woman reappeared a few seconds later and 'completed the passage behind the last pane very rapidly.'

A 'friar' is said to haunt a 16th century building in Beverley. The owner reported: 'From records of early sightings he appears to be a kindly old man with a funny haircut. I have had first-hand information about his appearances in upper rooms of the house. We understand that in its early days the property was a friary. There is a story that the old friar used to appear to a young boy who slept in the attic of the house and used to blow his candle out.'

Pickering Castle, dating from the 12th century, did not produce a ghost until 1950. A Ministry of Works custodian was sitting near the site of the drawbridge at about 7 p.m. one stormy evening when he saw the figure of a monk moving swiftly across the lawn from the steps of the keep to the site of the castle's ovens. The monk was tall, dressed in a long grey robe knotted at the waist with a girdle, and hooded so that the face could not be seen. The hands were outstretched as though he was carrying something.

A bridleway connects Malhamdale with Settle, passing near Pikedaw Hill and through Stockdale. Calamine was mined at Pikedaw and samples of the mineral can still be found on moorland spoil heaps. The caverns were 'rediscovered' by Craven potholers shortly after the 1939-45 war. A shallow pool is seen on the floor of one of the three main passages leading from a spoil heap at the foot of the entrance shaft. Near this pool the late Eli Simpson, one of the founders of the British Speleological Association, had an uncanny feeling. He sensed that someone was standing behind him, but there was no one there. Mr. Simpson was not easily shaken but he felt overawed at the experience.

A female member of the surveying party had the same disturbing sensation and she hurried to the foot of the entrance shaft where Mr. Simpson and others were preparing to ascend. Perhaps the ghost of a miner haunted the shallow muddy pool. The caverns form an eerie system where the dripping of water in unseen crevices is easily mistaken for tapping by a ghostly hammer or pick. Members of the B.S.A. were working in the caverns when they heard a distinct tapping sound. This time no ghost was involved; a member of the party was tapping in a higher series of caverns over a quarter of a mile away.

When Edward Garrett was a farm lad in Teesdale, he walked to the inn to buy some tobacco for his father. The figure of a small boy wearing fustian coat and red cap appeared ahead of him. The boy looked at Garrett, smiled — and vanished. A farm servant said it would be the ghost of Jack Stevens, who died rather horribly when he watched some men loading coal into a truck in the Cockfield area. Jack fell into the truck and was covered with coal. His body was found when the vehicle was emptied.

The library of York Museum was haunted in 1953 by an old man wearing a frock coat and drainpipe trousers. He had side whiskers. The apparition had a stoop and shuffling gait. He closely examined some of the books.

Halliwell Sutcliffe, writer of many West Riding novels, lived at Linton. Revelling in fantasy, he told an old story of an imp called Pam, who played at Threshfield school during the night. Sometimes Rector Smith wrote his sermons in the school. He left his manuscript on the desk on Saturday evening and had to return for it. Pam resented the intrusion and cuffed the Rector on the neck before bolting. The Rector knew that Pam enjoyed strong drink; he placed a bottle of brandy on the schoolmaster's desk and

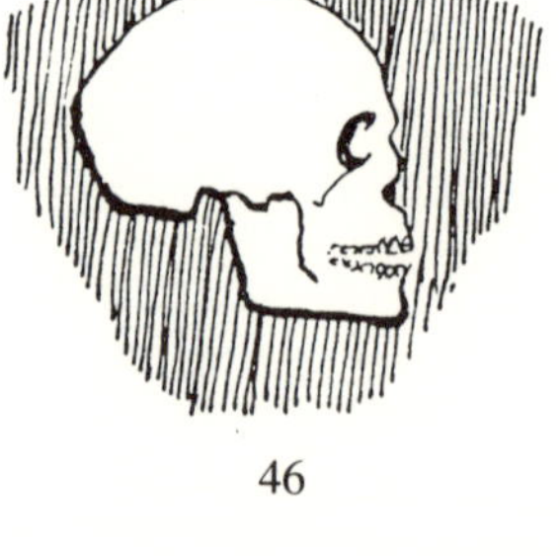

Pam became so drunk that he could not move. There are two versions of what befell the imp. In one account, the Rector killed the inebriated Pam and buried the body behind the school. The other story spares Pam and states that he annoyed the Rector to the end of his life.